TOO FLY NOT TO FLY

AN ALPHABET PHOTO BOOK BY
BRIANA McLean & DESMOND OWUSU

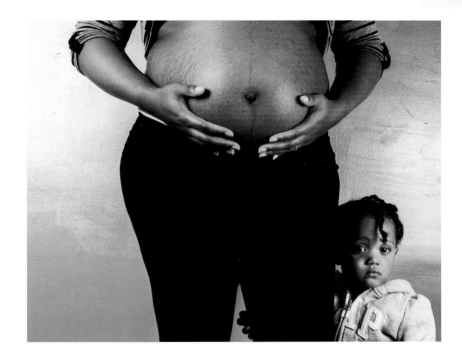

"God grant me wings.
I'm too fly not to fly."
-Saul Williams, The Dead Emcee Scrolls

Aa

A is for America.

Bb

B is for Beautiful.

C is for Color.

D is for Dream.

Ee

E is for Ebony.

F is for Fly.

Ff

Gg

G is for Grown.

Hh

H is for History.

Ii

I is for Inspire.

J j

J is for Joy.

Kk

K is for King.

L l

L is for Love.

Mm

M is for Magic.

N is for Nutrition.

Oo

O is for Obstacle.

P p

P is for Proud.

Qq

Q is for Queen.

Rr

R is for Roots.

S is for Strength.

Ss

Tt

T is for Together.

Uu

U is for Unity.

Vv

V is for Voice.

W is for Wings.

Ww

Xx

X is for eXplore.

Yy

Y is for Youth.

Zz

Z is for Zion.

The following questions are intended
to expand conversations in your
home or classroom around
the images featured in this book.

When reading with students, we encourage sharing your own connections to the questions. Modeling personal reflection of your experiences creates an open, honest and comfortable space of sharing for students!

America
1. Tell me about your favorite TV show or movie. How many characters in your favorite show or movie look like you?
2. When you watch shows or movies that you love, and you see characters that look like you, how does it make you feel?
3. When you watch shows or movies that you love and you *don't* see characters that look like you, how does it make you feel?

Beautiful
1. What makes someone beautiful?
2. Can one person be more beautiful than another person?

Color
1. What do you see when you look at this page?
2. Does everyone on this page have the same skin color?
3. Does everyone in your family have the same skin color? Do you have friends who have family members with a different skin color than their own?

Dream
1. What are some things you dream about?
2. Can you dream when you are awake?
3. What are some things you dream will happen in the future?

Ebony
1. Ebony is another word for dark brown or black. What are some things in our world that are the color "ebony"?
2. Sometimes people make judgements about other people JUST by looking at them. Has anyone ever judged you based on how you look? If so, how did that make you feel?
3. Do your feelings always show on your face? Do you always smile when you're happy? Do you always frown when you're sad?

Fly
1. Sometimes one word can mean two different things. When you tell someone they are "fly" you are giving them a compliment. Think of someone you think is cool or "fly". What makes them "fly"?
2. The word fly can also be something you do! When someone "flies" it can mean that they are accomplishing their goals. Goals are things you want to do! What are some goals you would like to accomplish in the future?

Grown
1. What does it mean to be grown?
2. What can adults do that kids can't? What can kids do that adults can't?
3. Would you rather be an adult or a kid? Why?

History
1. When something is history, it has already happened. Why is it important to know about things that happened in the past?
2. How does learning and discussing history help us to be better people and make better choices today?

Inspire
1. When someone inspires you, they make you feel good about who you are and who you want to become! Who inspires you in your life?
2. What do they do to make you feel inspired and good about yourself?
3. Is it important to inspire others? If so, why?

Joy
1. What is something that brings you joy and makes you happy?
2. What is something that takes that joy away?

King
1. Can anyone be a king?
2. How does a king show their leadership?
3. Do kings and people with power always use their power for good?

Love
1. Everyone has something that makes them special! What are some special things that you love about yourself?
2. Why is it important to love yourself?

Magic
1. What do you think of when you hear the word magic?
2. Have you ever had anything magical happen in your life?

Nutrition
1. What are some of your favorite foods? Are your favorite foods good for your body?
2. In your neighborhood, where can you buy sweet foods like candy and soda?
3. In your neighborhood, where can you buy healthy foods like fruits and vegetables?
4. In your neighborhood, is it easier to find healthy food or junk food?

Obstacle
1. An obstacle makes it difficult to get something you want. What is an obstacle you've faced when trying to get something you wanted?
2. Does everyone have the same obstacles?
3. How can an obstacle make you stronger?

Proud
1. What are some things that make you feel proud of who you are?
2. Tell me about something other than yourself that makes you feel proud.

Queen
1. If you were a queen for a day and you could change one thing about this world, what would it be?
2. Do queens have the same power as kings?
3. Do you think it's important for kings and queens to have the same power? Why?
4. Do you think boys and girls are treated the same? Why or why not?

Roots
1. The roots of plants help them to live a long and healthy life. Who in your life supports you and makes your life better?
2. What have you learned from the people in your family?
3. What are some things you love about the people in your family?

Strength
1. Think of someone who is really strong. What do they look like?
2. What are some things strong people do?
3. Is there more than one way to be strong?

Together
1. Working together is important but not always easy. What can be difficult when working with other people?
2. What good comes from working with other people?

Unity
1. Unity happens when people come together and support each other. Think about different communities of people like your classroom at school or a team of people playing a sport. Can you think of a time when a group you belonged to didn't support each other?
2. What happens to a group when people don't unite and work as a team? How would it feel to be a part of a divided group?

Voice
1. Can you think of a time when you were speaking and someone didn't listen? How did that make you feel?
2. Why is it important to listen when someone speaks?

Wings
1. Wings help birds and insects go places they want to go! What are some things in your life, that help you do what you want to do?
2. Who are the people in your life who help you do the things you want to do?
3. Do all people have support to do what they want to do?

eXplore
1. When we explore we are learning more about places or things! What is a place you would love to explore?
2. What is something you would love to explore and know more about?

Youth
1. Youth is another word for being a kid! There are one billion kids in the world. How are all kids the same? How are all kids different?
2. Does every kid have the same experience being a kid?

Zion
1. Just like the word fly, the word Zion has many meanings. Sometimes Zion means a place where you have everything you've ever wanted! If you could have one day to do everything you've ever wanted, what would that day look like? Where would you go? What would you do?

A big thank you to all the *fly* student collaborators for making this book possible…

Matthew Anderson
Nina Anderson
JaMere Beamon
Prince Beamon
Aaliyah Blumenberg
Jaylah Brewton
Jalen Brown
Cedrick DeBerry
Jakai Hayes
Christopher Hibbitt Jr.
A'Kasha Hodges

Ellis Humphries
Alexis Hunt
Mikayla Hurst
Sophia Hurst
Madeline Hurst
Christian Jackson
Kirsten Jackson
Kamarion Jones
Leniah LaCaze
Seriah LaCaze
Jamal LaCaze

Kentrell McNeal
Leilani Nichols
Cedelle Owusu
Zaria Owusu-Young
Zenaida Owusu-Young
Austin Pearl
Anarria Powell
Miracle Powell
Zoë Robinson
Jakyra Rodgers
Giselle Stevenson
Kaylen Woodard

…and the **Center for Restorative Solutions** for their continued support.